BUILDINGS

OF

ARRAN

BUILDINGS

OF

ARRAN

Arran Civic Trust

The Arran Civic Trust is affiliated to The Scottish Civic Trust. Its aims are to strive for excellence in environmental design. It hopes to preserve the quality and character of its surroundings in Arran against urban sprawl and encourage appropriate development.

Published by
Lavinia Gibbs, Secretary to the Arran Civic Trust

©Arran Civic Trust 2010

ISBN 978 0 9541851 2 1

Printed by Clydeside Press Ltd
37 High Street, Glasgow G1 1LX
clydesidepress@btconnect.com

Map of Arran by Latitude Mapping Ltd
www.latitudemaps.co.uk

Cover design by I. Lesley Hope Main, Main Fine Art©
www.mainfineart.com

ACKNOWLEDGEMENTS

Ian Ferguson suggested that the Arran Civic Trust should compile this guidebook, a proposal he has very ably carried forwards to its realisation. He has been assisted by a subcommittee, of whom Sally Campbell has been an outstandingly energetic member. The other members were Lavinia Gibbs, David Irwin and Michael Main.

Chrissie White, Grace Small and Members of The Arran Heritage Museum have assisted in checking the text and making valuable suggestions, for which we have been most grateful. John Campbell is thanked for his photography of many of the buildings and Lesley Main for her design of the cover.

In addition ACT would like to record their appreciation to all those who have shown an interest in the project and provided information.

A Community Development Grant from North Ayrshire Council's Community Development Grant Scheme for Arran and North Ayrshire is gratefully acknowledged.

Buildings of Arran was published with the generous assistance of a bequest from the late Mrs. Frances Margaret Handford, who had many happy memories of Arran

CONTENTS

FOREWORD

Perhaps the most thrilling view of Arran afforded by The National Trust for Scotland is the panorama provided by the tall arched windows in the Robert Adam's Round Drawing Room at Culzean, although quite often this massive island remains completely invisible when it withdraws into enveloping wreaths of soft grey Scotch mists.

This unusually extensive scale for a west coast island at an impressive 20 miles by roughly 10, in combination with the fact that almost the entire island was owned for centuries by Scotland's premier ducal Hamilton family, whose managers were under orders to use the latest experimental methods to make agricultural potential pay ever higher rents, could not but be conducive to the creation of purposeful buildings. This utilitarian stock of modern farm buildings joined a perhaps surprisingly high number of architecturally tentative early castles and churches in the Arran landscape, testifying to a more unsettled past. But given the island's ability to clutch at the heart-strings of day trippers like me, these dourer early monuments were soon to be joined by a diverse layer of cheerful recreational holiday architecture, with inns giving way to hotels and youth hostels for visitors and a myriad of villas for trippers who chose to stay.

I can vividly remember my first visit to Arran as an unashamed day-tripper. It was a perfect day so the operatic intensity of the island's dramatic silhouette was seen in all its craggy mountainous glory, bathed in early morning sun as the welcoming inward sweep of Brodick Bay embraced us. With time to spare, we were able to walk up to the Castle. The roadside verges were dew laden and the whole appeared to have been new-minted by God that very morning for our pleasure. Then came the fairytale Castle itself, whose ancient parts bore witness to Robert the Bruce and Scotland's early struggles for independence, but whose Victorian zones had been extended for a real flesh and blood Princess by James Gillespie Graham, a consummate master of picturesque scenography.

Taken as a group, however, it is the holiday villas which perhaps are the glory of Arran. Under initial estate control, the first few pioneers were perhaps indistinguishable from farmhouses but soon openly competed with the ducal patronage of the picturesque. With an optimistic confidence that the Scottish summer weather will change for the better, these villas delight in balconies, porches, and one ravishing cast-iron veranda but the hands down winner in the stakes of this genre being the improbably over-verandahed Drimla Lodge, more like a Mississippi paddle steamer than a house and whose charms would look a bit tamer in Sidmouth or Simla.

If the early tourism that is commemorated in these cycles of stretches of villadom has grown to the extent that it has now become the mainstay of the island's economy, Arran has impressive industrial archaeological record in its distillery, a barytes mine and more surprisingly the late 18th century Pirn Mill making bobbins for Paisley that shows how efficiently the Clyde shipping served the island.

Though perhaps more a function of the island conditions than industrialisation, Arran has a good collection of prefabricated or kit buildings like the pleasant former Pirnmill Free Church which are less likely to survive on the mainland. The skilful use of the same timber that underpinned the Clyde shipping, was a feature of the island's buildings and especially the distinctive backhouses at Hamilton Terrace which bring to mind rows of framehouses far away in Newport, Rhode Island. The modern villa of Greyholme happily preserves this timber tradition today. Everywhere corrugated iron replaced thatch and if it is sadly no longer possible to buy a stamp in 'the last thatched Post Office in Scotland' that lingered at Shannochie you can still happily post a letter in one of Britain's most monumental pillar boxes, like some Druid altar, that served Dougarie.

Moving inland, the whole history of farming can be traced in Arran's agricultural heritage from ancient times in the clachans, to the experimental improvements by the Hamilton estates in the Age of Enlightenment marked by the pneumatic increase in scale down the years. Since there was initially little incentive to add to the costs through imported materials, these early farm houses and buildings are stocky and plain and at one with the landscape, although thatch gave way to imported slates.

Arran possesses a quite spectacular number of churches as disagreements within the Established Church gave rise to schisms and fragmentation with the Free Church, swelled by legacies from the first generation of seceders, indulged architects to throw their weight around the landscape.

The Hamilton estates' patronage of the architect Sir John James Burnett, and the firm's private work locally, has left a rich legacy of fetching Arts and Crafts churches, terraces of houses and villas with a no less plentiful show of timber which gives a sophisticated twist to these handicraft traditions.

This attractive architectural guide cannot but tempt us to explore Arran's rich and varied stock of distinctive buildings.

IAN GOW Chief Curator of The National Trust for Scotland
February 2010

BRODICK CASTLE

LOCHRANZA CASTLE

PREAMBLE

This Arran Civic Trust publication is a guide to the most interesting and significant buildings on Arran and has been compiled for the enjoyment of residents and visitors alike.

The Guide is an exploration of the island's buildings, intended for those who visit and tour by car, as well for the more energetic who prefer to walk or cycle. While not comprehensive it does give details of the attractive and significant buildings which can be seen from public roads. It is hoped that, by including blank pages at the end, readers can be persuaded to add their suggestions and corrections where their researches have been more profound than those of the authors. However, a word of caution, the buildings selected can only be viewed from a public road or other public space. It is important that visitors do not intrude upon private property.

This is a clockwise guide around the island starting at Brodick Castle, the most iconic building on the island. The route follows the main road around the island. There are additional notes on buildings to be found on the two cross routes, the String and Ross roads and on the Machrie Moor road linking the 'Celtic pillar box' to Machrie.

INTRODUCTION

The Isle of Arran has been owned in the past by successive Dukes of Hamilton for over four hundred years. The Dukes and their factors (managers) decided what was built, where it was built, the height of the building and how it was built. The design and materials were also decided by the Estate. So the built environment of Arran was largely decided by the feudal landowner. The ancient Celtic land systems of clachans and runrig gradually came under their control. The only exception was the small area of land owned by the Fullartons, who built Kilmichael in Brodick on land given to the family by King Robert III in 1400.

Although not spectacular as regards its built heritage, Arran's interest lies in its huge variety of building styles. The encouragement to settle started early. In the latter part of the 18th century, during the time of Burrel (Appendix 2), the surveyor appointed to the estate of the Duke of Hamilton carried out a review of the agriculture of whole island with a view to increasing productivity and increasing income; the estate in the 1770s began encouraging better-off families to build large houses, such as Seafield on the Clauchlands Road in Lamlash and Cromla in Corrie, on 99 year leases. Burrel was instrumental in directing the estate to reorganize the farms into larger units and the estate wished to attract capital to run these units by constructing impressive farmhouses.

It is important to understand how different Arran would have looked before the Clearances (see Appendix 1) conducted by Bauchope (see Appendix 2) in 1820 and later. Agricultural improvements resulted in larger farms, more industrial agricultural practices and greater numbers of sheep and game; as a consequence there was a great displacement of people from their homes and settlements. Trade at that time was also having an impact, such as quarrying, mining and fishing.

The agricultural changes that were made gradually replaced the clachans (see Appendix 1). They predate the clearances of 1820-30. These, part of the ancient Celtic communal farms, were villages which had no streets, the buildings being clustered seemingly at random. Of these, the only one left largely intact is High Corrie. Here the gables of the original "black houses" were partly rebuilt to take chimneys, some windows were enlarged, the dry stone walls were pointed up with mortar and tarry felt replaced the original thatched roofs. Elsewhere on the island very little of the old Arran can be observed. There are no black houses, although their descendants in the 17th and 18th century cottages can be seen; these are often characterized by sloping with the contours of the land and with low roofs and small, square windows set into thick, rough walls of boulders. These houses were originally thatched, this being replaced eventually by felt or small Scottish slates or simply covered over with corrugated iron.

During the late 18th and early 19th centuries small clachans were consolidated and much larger single farms were built to increase productivity and financial returns through new and more productive agricultural practices. Farms acquired more familiar appearances, with individual farmhouses and steadings forming compact groups in the landscape. Most of the clearing on Arran was to make way for larger arable and cattle farms. By the end of the 19th century even the new, ordinary farmhouses had become bigger and were of Georgian proportions with large symmetrically placed windows. 'Buildings of the Scottish Countryside' (Naismith, 1985) illustrates this system clearly. But detailing was still of the simplest, the only distinctive features being the 'skewed' gables and banded windows (the skews are those parts of the gable walls which project above the roof line). When the larger houses began to be built, styles varied widely. Dougarie Lodge, the principal hunting lodge of the Hamiltons, was a highly romantic effusion of gables and towers owing much to Walter Scott, whilst Strabane and the Auchrannie are more severe. Seafield in Lamlash, meanwhile, is a simply proportioned Georgian building dating from the late 1770s, as are the manses at St. Bride's, Lamlash, and Kilmory.

Later, during the late 19th and early 20th centuries, as tourism began to develop, the resulting holiday villas and boarding houses adopted a similar pattern: constructed in sandstone, large-windowed, heavy substantial structures, evidence of the wealth of Glasgow at that period. Whiting Bay was feued in the late 1880s. Many of the farmhouses, which had been built originally in an older fashion, were modernised. Their walls were heightened to create bedrooms upstairs, dormer windows built in the new slated roofs and windows enlarged downstairs. This building boom was given a further impetus during the 20th century by the construction of new piers in Brodick, Lamlash and Whiting Bay, the island being served by regular ferry services from Largs, Fairlie, Campeltown and Glasgow. Yet, despite increasing uniformity, variation existed between the different villages and settlements; dormer windows in Lochranza tend to be octagonal-sided, whereas those in Brodick are without angled sidelights, their places taken by slated 'haffits' (dormer sides). Not all the villas from this period were utilitarian in architectural appearance. Heathfield in Corrie, for example, shows the playful use of bargeboards, cross-ties and verticals in its dormers.

During the time when holiday accommodation became fashionable, when houses were not necessarily part of a farm complex, these comparatively grand villas were sited to take advantage of good views in proximity to the sea, as, for example, in Lochranza and later in Whiting Bay. Also during this period, islanders capitalised upon the tourist trade by building back houses, small dwellings to the rear of their property to which they could retreat during the summer, enabling them to rent the main house to visitors. Examples of these can be glimpsed in almost every village.

To summarise, most of what you see today is not the residue of the old clachans with their distinctive and now forgotten ways of life but rather the additions and refinements over more than two centuries of 'improvement' resulting in sweeping changes to agricultural practice in the 19th century. The later growth of tourism and its attendant commerce in the forms of hotels, boarding and back houses came with the piers and regular ferry services. The visitor can enjoy the often beautiful settings of the villages and their individual dwellings which reflect the more recent history of Arran, and hint at a life long since departed.

IAN FERGUSON Editor
February 2010

BRODICK

'Old' Brodick consisted of the castle and associated villages of Cladach below and Dykehead above. 'New' Brodick, centred round Invercloy, was created by the heir to the 10th Duke of Hamilton, afterwards the 11th Duke, to provide greater privacy for himself and his bride, the Princess Marie of Baden.

BRODICK CASTLE

Since the Viking period which effectively ended in 1263, there has always been a building on this site. Its strategic position on the island contributed greatly to the defence of the Clyde estuary in mediaeval times. In the late 16th century a rectangular, baronial style tower was built for the deposed regent Lord Arran. In the middle of the 17th century, Cromwellian troops added a battery to the east and extensions to the west. Improvements were made in the early 18th century, but it is the additions which were made in the 19th century by the architect James Gillespie Graham which now dominate the building. The Earls, later Dukes, of Hamilton owned the Castle and most of the Island for over four centuries. Brodick Castle, its contents and its gardens passed to the National Trust for Scotland in 1958. Description of the history and contents of the Castle can be found in National Trust of Scotland publications.

NOTE: The Castle and Gardens open Easter to the end of October. Country Park open all year round

In the Castle grounds, see the fine bottle-shaped **Ice House** and **Bavarian Summer House**, built to help make the Princess Marie, consort of the 11th Duke, feel less homesick. The interior was renovated by school pupils from the Isle of Wight.

Beside the car park, the **Visitors' Centre** was built in 1992 to designs by the architects Page and Park.

Approaching the **Ranger's Centre**, reached via a short access leading off the main drive opposite the Castle's disabled access spur, see the row of cottages on the right hand side. Originally thatched this was built as a pastiche to resemble a typical 'thatched row'. Note that it is often possible to determine whether cottages have been thatched by looking at the eaves line: if this is not parallel with the line of slates, which require a squared up roof, the probability is that the roof was previously thatched.

CASTLE RANGERS COTTAGES

Descending the back drive, note on the right the fine mid-19th century former gamekeeper's house and kennels for the Castle. Its design resembles that of Brodick School and Alma Terrace.

CLADACH

The settlement of Cladach lies to the west of the sawmill and opposite the car park. Central to Cladach is the well-proportioned 18th century **former inn**, now part of the Wineport restaurant complex. Built by the Duchess Ann (1635-1716) for her physician, it was roofed in Lochranza slates and hence was known as Tigh Sgleat. Apart from the Castle, it was the first house in Brodick to be slated. The building is of historical importance in that Burrel, the surveyor to the Estate (see Appendix 2), used it as a place to meet island representatives to discuss such matters as the provision of a 'pacquet boat' (ferry) to serve the Island and the new farming methods which he was proposing to introduce. The building featured in the Glasgow Journal as early as 1759 and continued to serve as an inn until the mid-1850s. It was converted into apartments and provided accommodation for estate employees until well into the 20th century.

OLD INN

Although little remains of the former buildings in Cladach, their general arrangement can still be appreciated. Beyond the Wineport Restaurant, which occupies the first of the cottages, there used to exist the old **Courthouse**, where the Baron-Baillies dealt with all but the most serious offences. An attractive building possessing a stone belfry, it collapsed whilst undergoing renovation in the early 2000s. During the mid-19th century, the court was transferred to a new, sandstone building on a site behind the Springbank Inn (now the Douglas Hotel q.v.). In the 1980s, this became the Roman Catholic Chapel.

The old saddle room, loose boxes and castle laundry once occupied the site of the present brewery and there was a fine timber coach house, now also demolished, situated near the detached stone villa to the west.

Other buildings of interest are the **Power House** (Hydro Electric Station), which once housed a Pelton Wheel fed by a 7 1/2" (190 mm) diameter pipe from a feeder pond 225 metres above the Castle near the lower deer fence. In about 1912, the Marquis of Graham had the plant installed to provide electricity for the Castle, estate offices, stables, workshops, sawmill and joiner's shop. The building and system have been refurbished to once again provide electricity by hydro-power.

It is likely that the Power House occupies the site of the old **Meal Mill**, recorded by Burrel. In former times it was usual for a feudal superior, or the landowner of a substantial estate, to erect at his own expense a mill for grinding grain. His tenants had to take their grain to his mill and pay for it to be ground. In 1776, seventy families were thus 'thirled' to the Cladach mill and 942 pecks of grain were ground. In 1862 the mill was replaced by a new one at Monamhor, Lamlash.

Adjacent to the Power House is the **Sawmill**, originally run by the Estate, and nearby are craft workers' workshops and the new mountain rescue centre.

In about 1810 the **landing place** for Brodick was moved from Cladach to the quay at the burn below the Springbank Inn, before this in turn was replaced by the **New Pier** in 1872. The small, sandstone harbour along from the sawmill towards Corrie provided access for castle visitors and goods. Set into the wall opposite the quay is the plaque commemorating the arrival on Arran in 1902 of the new king Edward VII and his consort, Queen Alexandra. From this point commence the milestones, small sandstone obelisks marking distances around the Island in a clockwise direction.

TOWARDS BRODICK

'Old' Brodick lies to the west, separated from Cladach by the burn. This area was known as Mossend. Within Mossend lay Old Brodick, of which '**The Street**' opposite Duchess Court (Home Farm) formed the principal access. The first group of buildings, now housing the Duchess Court shops and Arran Aromatics, was at one time the **Home Farm**. During World War One 1914-18 (WW1) there was a need for food to be home grown and estate land was brought into cultivation for that purpose. It was established as a 'model farm' whose Red Poll cattle were much prized by the then Duchess and Jean Gordon, the dairymaid.

Opposite the farm and along 'The Street' stood the village of **Old Brodick,** created in Burrel's time to house tenants moved from Cladach and lying within the land known as Mossend. This area ended at the standing stone at Rosaburn. All that remains now is the beige/orange cottage adjacent to the road which was then the village inn. The settlement was cleared in about 1856.

At the bend in the road, a hundred yards beyond Duchess Court, is the entrance to **Strabane**. The house is private and invisible except in part from the golf course. It was constructed in 1823 on the site of a farmhouse for a Dr. John Stoddart, before being acquired and altered for his successor, Patrick Murray, the Duke's chamberlain. The farmhouse was incorporated into the new building, the architect for the alterations being George Paterson of the Hamilton Estates Office.

At the junction with the String Road (q.v.), a field entrance on the right leads into Douglas Park and the Arran Estates Office.

Previously this was the manse to the Glen Rosa Established Church, now demolished; before that the home of the Castle piper, Michael McCarfrae. The church was built in 1839, but at the 'Disruption' in 1843, when the Free Church separated from the main body, a new Free Church was built in Corriegills in about 1847. The building you see, dating from the late 19th century, incorporates certain features typical of the Aesthetic Movement and in particular of the architect W.E. Nesfield. He is known to have completed some design work for the Duke of Hamilton. It is worth comparing it stylistically with the gatehouse to the former White House in Lamlash and to the Lamlash Church Parish Hall. Note the graveyard some yards up the String Road on the right hand side.

ARRAN ESTATES OFFICE

Make a short diversion up the road to Glen Rosa to view over the left-hand boundary wall the old **Mill House**. In 1861, after the 'steading' (the barns, stables and outbuildings of a farm) had reverted to the Estate, a Carding Mill was built on this site, replacing one at Mossend. It ceased activity in 1905. Of interest is that in June 1861 Robert Davidson received £27.12.0 (£27.60) for carting stones for the erection of the mill and John Hendry £20.1.2 (£20.11) for making the wheel.

MILL HOUSE

Returning to the main road, continue on towards Brodick. On the left stand two houses in mock Renaissance style. The first of these is modern but the second, **Rosaburn Lodge**, is one of two houses designed by the architect-owner Thomson in the 1950s in the east coast, Scottish vernacular style. The second example of his work, 'The Sheeans', may be seen on Strathwillan Road.

Next to Rosaburn Lodge stands the **Isle of Arran Heritage Museum**. This was formed partly out of the 18th century school, petitioned in 1779 at the Rosaburn according to Burrel's Journal. The museum is an eclectic mix of buildings, including a working 'smiddy' (blacksmith's shop) and various cottages, giving a microcosm of the types of improved farm buildings and equipment found on Arran during the 19th century. Note the vivid colours of the window frames with bands typical of cottages at that time.

Further along on the right stands **Brodick School,** now the primary school. This was built in 1854 and opened in 1856 in a style similar to Alma Terrace (q.v.). It replaced the small schoolroom at the Museum and was the gift of the 11th Duke of Hamilton, whose wife the Princess Marie was involved in improving education on the Island. His statue stands in the playground. Note the mock-Tudor detailing of the bargeboards, chimneys and window arch heads.

Opposite the school, set back in wooded gardens behind the standing stone, is a large timber house, **Greyholme**, designed by the architect owner Gibson during the 1930s. Its easterly aspect may be glimpsed from the golf course.

GREYHOLME

At the corner of the school playground, walk along **Douglas** Place, formerly New Street. This striking terrace was built in 1856 to provide accommodation for Estate employees. Its most notable feature is the shared common drying green, which provides the simply designed buildings with a pleasant setting and the cultivation plots beyond. A curiosity was the pattern of ownership: each house was allocated the bank to the rear on which it was permitted to build a back house, a small dwelling to which the owner would retreat to free the main house for summer letting. The rear access, however, together with the relevant part of the front green were feued to Arran Estates and the narrow access strip before the front doors to members of the Hamilton family. It is said that the Princess Marie had a hand in the design, since there were various details reminiscent of continental practice such as inward opening windows. Of interest on the ground floor of one of the houses is a window with three horizontal sliding sashes, a type rarely found in Scotland. The vertical sliding sashes elsewhere are later replacements.

DOUGLAS PLACE

DOUGLAS PLACE

Returning to the main road, several houses on the right between the school and the Orwin Hotel were built in 1835. The **Orwin** itself, formerly Low Glencloy Cottage, served for a time as Brodick post office and shop, prior to it moving to Invercloy.

A hundred metres further on and just before the bridge, turn up the side road towards the **Auchrannie Hotel**. The road is undistinguished except for **Oakbank**, hidden behind extensive planting 100 metres along on the right hand side. Originally with extensive grounds, it was built in 1883 of red sandstone by the McBride family of Glencloy to replace a thatched cottage and was extended in Edwardian times. The windows are original, as are the ornate bargeboards over the dormer windows. **Auchrannie** was built by the son of a Rothesay man called Fullarton and called after the area. The Dowager Duchess of Hamilton bought it in 1928 and it was altered for her use by the architect George Williamson. It is similar in style to Strabane (q.v.). Sandstone was imported for the frontage. After she died in 1934 it was sold and opened as a hotel by Ian Kerr. The house's development into a large hotel complex has taken place since the 1980s.

Back on the main road, turn right just across the bridge into the Knowe Road. The first building of note is the **Parish Church**, (1910), whose architects were D. and J. McMillan of Aberdeen. It is built in Gothic style of a pleasing scale and simplicity in keeping with the Edwardian period. Next door, the **Church Hall** is a delightful corrugated structure, which served at one time as the United Free Church at Bennicarrigan, near Kilmory.

BRODICK CHURCH HALL

The **Ormidale Hotel** stands on the left in its own grounds, beyond the all-weather pitch. It was built for George Hering, Baron von Heringen, and his family about 1855, who adopted a 'daughter' of the Hamilton family known as the 'wee girl', re-named by them Jeanie Hering.

Beyond the Knowe Road end, come to the **Kilmichael House Hotel**. This stands on land granted to the Fullartons by King Robert III in 1400 and is a plain but satisfying early Georgian laird's house dating from the 18th century. Its principal rooms were on the first floor, the ground floor being given over to servants and services. The lower ceilings and smaller windows on the ground floor are an indicator of an earlier construction, but overall its fine proportions and rarity in west Scotland make it well worth a visit.

KILMICHAEL HOUSE

On the main road again and approaching Invercloy, on the left stands **Brodick Public Hall**. Built to a fine Arts and Crafts design by J.J. Burnett (Appendix 3), it opened in 1895. It was paid for by public subscription, the lease of the site being granted by the Duke of Hamilton. The original plans showed a clock tower, but this was not included in the cost of the final scheme, which was £1,400 (£120,000 in today's money).

BRODICK PUBLIC HALL

BRODICK PUBLIC HALL DOOR

INVERCLOY

Just beyond the bowling green is the **pharmacy**. Originally, this was the post office and was built in 1886 for Ernest Ribbeck to replace the one he had run 'up the lane' since 1870 at the back of the new village of Invercloy. After serving as the post office, the building was used for some years as the golf club house before its final metamorphosis into the pharmacy. Internally there still remain some of the golf club boxes.

PHARMACY

Walking along the street, come first to the Bank of Scotland building with its turreted feature. An office stood on this site from 1888 and in 1926-7 the premises were enlarged and a dwelling house attached. **Eilean Mhor,** formerly Stalkers, occupies the oldest building in Invercloy (1809). **Invercloy House**, just beyond, has Alexanders shop on its ground floor. The building dates from about 1870 and was built for Henry Ribbeck. It was called originally 'Germania', since the Ribbeck brothers emigrated from

Germany to Scotland at about the same time as the Princess Marie of Baden.

Across the road from Brodick pier, the imposing red sandstone **Douglas Hotel** was built in 1856-8 to replace the Springbank Inn, which was inadequate to accommodate the increasing number of visitors who preferred living in hotels and villas rather than simple cottages and inns. It was erected on the site of a steading, Springbank, which had a separate lease. Hector McAlister's Villa was built on one acre which had a 99 year lease and was included as part of the hotel. After Hector McAlister, the lessee was Peter McDonald and later the Public House Trust. Combined with the St. Denys Hotel behind, it was extended several times. Now in 2010 it is undergoing a further reincarnation as a 'boutique' hotel.

DOUGLAS HOTEL

Proceed towards the pier and to the rear of the small car park note the old **Piermaster's House**, built in 1872. This still retains its original front door and windows, unusual on the island today. Inside the pier terminal building there is a plaque commemorating the visit to the Island in 1947 of King George VI, Queen Elizabeth, the Princesses Elizabeth and Margaret and Lieutenant Philip Mountbatten. Originally, the plaque was sited in the old ticket office, an attractive small building attributed to J.J. Burnett and constructed in 1899. It was demolished by Caledonian McBrayne, despite efforts to save it, to make way for the new, more practical terminal. It was the fight to save this old ticket office that led to the formation of the Arran Civic Trust in 1993.

OLD TICKET OFFICE

OLD PIER 1901 BY STEWART ORR

Retracing your steps towards the Co-op, turn up Alma Road beside it and round the bend at the top. In addition to offering wide views over the village and bay, the road takes you past **Alma Terrace**, built in 1856 shortly after the conclusion of the Crimean War, hence the name. Resembling some contemporary English alms-houses, its purpose was to house tenants displaced from Mossend (q.v.). Others tenants were accommodated in Douglas Place (q.v.) and Invercloy.

ALMA TERRACE

STRATHWHILLAN AND CORRIEGILLS

Brief diversions may be made to **Strathwhillan** - turn left about two hundred metres up the pier brae - and to **Corriegills,** a further two hundred metres.

Just before reaching the Strathwhillan road end, note **Strathwhillan House**, built for Dr. Andrew Stoddart, son to the one who commissioned Strabane (q.v.) and, at the road end itself, houses of prefabricated construction built for Hydro Board employees in 1947. Further along the road and partly concealed by planting stands **The Sheeans**, the second house designed by Thomson of Rosaburn (q.v.). Towards the end of the road there is **Brandon Farm**, built in 1863 for a Mr. McDonald, lessee of the Springbank Inn, now the Douglas Hotel.

THE SHEEANS

Continuing along the main road towards the Corriegills turning, pass on the left **Carrick Lodge**. This was the former Manse, constructed in 1891 for the 'new' Free Church in Corriegills, the church itself being demolished a few years after the end of World War Two 1939-45 (WW2) (see Douglas Park). Corriegills possesses some attractive cottages and, beyond the bridge in **Dunfion**, a former 19th century farm complex, recently converted to three separate dwellings.

LAMLASH

The name 'Lamlash' is a corruption of St. Molaise (see **Holy Island**). It was adopted for the village during the 18th century.

Shortly after descending the hill from Brodick and past the golf club, turn left across the golf course and left again into the cemetery. Within the old cemetery lies **St. Bride's Chapel**, of which only the ruins remain. These ruins date back to the Scottish Reformation (1560) and contain the graves and tombstones of a number of old Arran families including the Fullartons. It is currently undergoing basic preservation work. Nearby stands **Kilbride House**, built during the latter half of the 18th century. Typically Georgian in style, this was the manse for Kilbride Parish, one of two parishes on the Island, the other being Kilmory.

ST. BRIDE'S CHAPEL

Return to the main road, descend to the foot of the hill where the road turns sharp right, but turn left into Clauchlands Road. There are a number of interesting buildings along the first half mile or so of this road, the first being the **North Ayrshire Council Offices**. This building was the school for the village between 1876 and 1946. **St. George's Church**, now disused and in a poor state of repair, was built for the Free Church of Scotland, the first service being held there in 1892. A little further, **Seafield**, a fine Georgian seaside villa with palm trees in the front garden, was built in c.1770 for the Croil family who were given a 99 year lease on the land. Rounding the bend in the road, past a small cottage and about a hundred metres further on, see on the left **Broich**, originally known as New Lanark. This was built in 1840 and is a good example of a double-fronted villa of the period. It was owned during the 1940s by Donald McKelvie, the 'potato king', who developed such famous varieties as Arran Pilot, Arran Banner and Arran Victory. It was a condition of its construction that it was set back forty metres from the road so as not to intrude upon the privacy of the Duke as he rode past.

SEAFIELD

31

BROICH

Return to the road junction. Immediately on the right on high ground stands **Kinneil House**, built for Captain Buchanan in 1885. The house was named after a 16th century residence of the Dukes of Hamilton near Bo'ness. Buchanan was a significant figure in Arran's history, since he was the master of the first steamer allowed to operate a ferry to the mainland and the only ferry owner to build a house on Arran. Interesting features of the house, which is privately owned and converted to holiday flats, include a large stained glass window on the main staircase which includes the depiction of the paddle steamer 'Brodick Castle' and a small window in the north gable through which the captain could observe, by telescope, shipping in the Firth of Clyde.

WINDOW illustrating PS 'BRODICK CASTLE'

100 metres along the main road on the left, at the parking area for the Drift Inn, stands the **Clock Tower**. This building was a depot for goods in transit to and from the mainland, the waiting room and pier offices being located in 'Seagates', the small building opposite. The clock tower, which had fine, wooden-panelled interiors, marks the site of the **New Pier**, built in about 1885 and closed in 1957 before being later demolished. The pier further west is known as the **Old Pier**.

On the right and partly facing you 100 metres after the pier approach road, is one of J.J. Burnett's most sensitive creations, the **'Made in Arran' craft shop**. It was designed in the late 1800s and retains some original detailing including the stairs.

MADE IN ARRAN CRAFT SHOP

The shop forms the first in a short terrace of finely proportioned and detailed former shops and boarding houses ending in the Glenisle Hotel. Just beyond the hotel and set back behind a green lies **Hamilton Terrace**. This impressive Arts and Crafts row was built to designs by J.J. Burnett in 1893, on the instructions of the Princess Marie of Baden, to replace terraced cottages known as the Old Row, which lay along the road frontage. Note the typical bay and dormer windows, some of which have been replaced. At the west end, providing an effective visual stop, is the post office. The houses were advanced for their day, being equipped with indoor water closets beside the back doors usable by occupants of both the front and back houses (see below). The kitchen ranges had ovens on one side and tanks on the other with taps providing hot water. Washing, both of the occupiers and their possessions, took place in the scullery. Outside, standpipes were provided at intervals in addition to a cold tap in the scullery.

HAMILTON TERRACE

Walk round the back of the row and see the equally striking **Hamilton Terrace Back Houses**, a charming series of virtually identical timber-fronted cottages. These were similar in concept if not in construction to the Old Row and possessed dry closets at the rear and wash boilers for laundry. It was a condition imposed by the Estate that each cottage should take no longer than a year to build after occupation of the front houses to which they were related.

BACK-HAMILTON TERRACE

At the road junction beyond Gordon's Stores, formerly The Ship Hotel, turn right and then left into Park Terrace, formerly Nicol Street and originally a thatched row (see the painting in Lamlash Parish Church). Just beyond the builder's offices see **Rose Cottage ('The Nurse's House')** and, next to it, **Dalgorm**, both designed by J.J. Burnett in 1899. Rose Cottage is dated 1900 on the building. Note the Arts and Crafts detailing and designs typical of Burnett's Arran work at this time.

ROSE COTTAGE

DALGORM

Behind the builder's offices is **Claveron**, a fine villa built in 1866, about the same time as Lamlash Parish Church, by Thomas MacNeish the postmaster. Some of the research into the pollination of potatoes was carried out by Donald McKelvie (see 'Broich') in the large greenhouse in the grounds.

CLAVERON

Further along the road, pass on the right the **Masonic Hall**, provided by the Hamilton Estate during WW1 to be used as an Anglican church.

Apart from a bullet dent left in the Lamlash Parish Church weathercock as a result of commando target practice, **Lamlash Village Hall** is the last remaining built reminder of Arran's contribution to both world wars. The Ardrossan and Saltcoats Herald of June 1914 noted that the Hall "is a large canteen establishment to be built by the Admiralty to provide accommodation for men's reading rooms, dressing rooms, refreshment rooms, canteen, manager's quarters, stores, picket room and lavatories etc. while provision is also being made for a stage and gymnasium and a veranda will run the full length of the buildings on one side. The contract (has been) placed with Messrs Spears (Ltd) Glasgow... work to be completed in two months." The building is a further good example of the portable corrugated iron structures seen elsewhere on the Island (Pirnmill Free Church and Brodick Church Hall q.v.) and provides the largest open floor area for public use on Arran. After the end of WW1, it was gifted to the community by the Admiralty on the understanding that it would be returned to them in the event of hostilities recurring. During WW2 it served as a naval centre, thus adding to its historical significance. There are current concerns about the future of this building.

LAMLASH VILLAGE HALL

LAMLASH VILLAGE HALL

Returning to the main street, the first building of importance is **Lamlash Parish Church**, formerly known as Kilbride Parish Church. Both Church and **Church Hall** were built in 1886 to designs by the architects H. and D. Barclay. To the left hand side at the rear note the small round structure with a conical roof. This was the minister's 'dry closet' (toilet).

LAMLASH CHURCH DRY CLOSET

LAMLASH CHURCH HALL

Adjacent to the church, set in wooded grounds, stood **The White House**, constructed during the 1760s, extended during the 19th century and let out by the Estate as a shooting lodge. A large building is described in Burrell's Journal, which suggests an earlier date. During part of that time it was occupied by the Dowager Duchess of Hamilton and in 1861 by an estate factor (manager). During WW2 it became the headquarters of 11th Scottish Commando before succumbing to dry rot and the bulldozer during the 1980s. Only the **Gatehouse**, with stylistic similarities to the Douglas Park Estate Office, and surrounding wall remain.

Beyond the White House used to stand the **High School**, replaced in 2008 by the new building visible beyond the car park designed by Keppie Design of Glasgow. The old school was constructed in 1939 but was requisitioned immediately as a naval barracks and Church of Scotland canteen. It reverted to its intended purpose in 1946 as Lamlash Junior Secondary School. Originally this school provided education only to the age of 14, after which children had to travel to the mainland to be taught at Rothesay or Ardrossan. It became the island's High School during the 1960s. Over the bridge turn left for a brief look at **Cordon**.

CORDON

Cordon is one of three remaining coastal clachans (Appendix 1) and was originally accessed across a ford. It retains several rows of cottages differing in style dating from the 19th century. At one time there was a large sandstone quarry in Cordon, one of three on the Island. Arran Heritage Museum possesses a sequential photographic record of one of the Cordon rows, showing the sea-facing gables and roofs being upgraded gradually from thatch to the more durable slate. The last cottage to be improved was owned by Coats, the thread company in Paisley, who let it to employees for holidays.

Returning to the main road, turn left towards Whiting Bay. On the right as you move out of the village stands a terrace of cottages, **Murray Place**, built in 1897 to re-house the tenants of Nicol Street, now Park Terrace.

Just before the road turns left up the hill, at the Ross Road end, note Arran Provisions. This occupies the site of the old **Meal Mill**, which worked until the 1920s and was demolished during the 1960s. Part of the basement of the Mill survives as the Arran Provisions Factory Shop.

HOLY ISLAND

The Island is now the property of the Samye Ling Buddhist Community but visiting is permitted. The 'holiness' of the Island derives from St. Molaise, an Irish missionary, Abbot of Leinster and one of Columba's disciples, who lived there until his death in 639. His cave with carved markings and a preaching stone may be found on the shore walk facing Arran. Near the landing stage, is the substantial headquarters of the community, incorporating a former

18th century farmhouse and steading dating from Burrel's time. There are two lighthouses, the one opposite Kingscross being built in 1877, engineered by Thomas and David Stevenson and the other, the Pillar facing across the Firth of Clyde, built in 1905, designed by Thomas Stevenson. He was Engineer to the Board of Northern Lighthouses at that time and father of Robert Louis Stevenson.

NOTE: Ferries serve Holy Island from the pier in Lamlash from Easter to October with timetable and booking at the cabin by the pier.

KINGSCROSS

Leave Lamlash, drive up the hill and across the top until, on the left, you see the sign for **Kingscross**.

There is little of note here, but a short distance from the road end see **Birchdean**, a traditional villa with outbuildings and back house, still relatively unchanged. The back house served as the local post office until 1978 but has since been modernised and converted for residential use. Mail, keepers' wages and provisions for the Holy Island 'Kingscross' lighthouse were received here.

WHITING BAY

Whiting Bay, Arran's third largest village, comprises a number of scattered settlements: from the north, **Auchencairn** and **Knockenkelly** on the higher ground, **Sandbraes** on the shore and spread along the bay, **North, Mid** and **South Kiscadale**. The clachans of **Largiemeanoch** and **Largybeg** lie further on towards Kildonan. The village as an entity did not exist before the 19th century and there are few buildings surviving prior to that date. Whiting Bay's role as a popular holiday resort developed slowly during the latter part of the 19th century, when the new shore road was built, and reached its heyday during the 1920s and 1930s. Much of the present character of the village reflects this.

For those wishing to follow the old road, as you descend the hill from Kingscross turn up towards **Auchencairn.** This road is the original one connecting the various settlements and remains much as it was when built by hand by the tenant population. Tenants were required by the Estate to set aside a certain number of days for the construction and maintenance of roads. Tracks leading up from the shore and from Sandbraes to Smiddy Brae and the School and Middle Roads are still passable on foot. Similar tracks, now paved, served South Kiscadale. There are few buildings of interest along the road other than a surviving Arran long house, **Broomhill Cottage**, which may be viewed across a field.

For visitors following the main road, upon entering the village come first to **Sandbraes** at the turning on the left. Note the **Stewart Memorial Church** standing behind the playing fields. It was built in 1910 and an angle-buttressed tower provides a fine visual end-stop to a hall-form interior with wood-lined roof. The church takes its name from the Reverend Angus Stewart, a late 19th century United Free Church minister to whose memory the tower was dedicated. The manse was constructed ten years after the church itself.

The row of houses between the main road and the church dates to before the 19th century, although the individual dwellings have been much modified since. The last cottage in the row, nearest the main road, gives the best idea of the row's original appearance. It retained its thatched roof until the 1970s when it was replaced with corrugated iron.

Proceeding along the main road, notice **Loudoun** and **Invermay**, the former built between 1881-91 and a good example of a modest Arran villa of that period. Invermay is more interesting. It is a substantial Arts and Crafts villa built c.1900. Its design may have originated in the office of J.J. Burnett, but if not it was heavily influenced by the office's style.

SANDBRAES ROW

INVERMAY

The hotels and guest-houses lying along the stretch beyond the Bay Stores date from 1900-10 and testify to Whiting Bay's role as a holiday resort. Built in a variety of styles, they reflect Arts and Crafts influences. Of particular interest are the **Trafalgar** and **Argentine Hotels**, the latter constructed in 1905 by a family with links to Argentina, and the **Burlington** and **Cameronia** dating from the same time. The Cameronia served briefly as the village post office during WW2.

As one moves from Sandbraes towards Kiscadale, pass the **Royal Arran Hotel** ('The Royal'). This well known village landmark dates from 1900, the land on which it stands having been purchased from the Duke of Hamilton in 1899. It was originally **Bannatyne's Temperance Hotel** and during WW2 served as a NAAFI for the Commandos, following which it became the village's first licensed bar.

ROYAL ARRAN HOTEL

46

Just beyond **Whiting Bay Primary School**, listed by Historic Scotland for its flamboyant design typical of the 1960s, stands the former **Established Church**, built in 1873. After it ceased functioning as a church it became first an art gallery, then a private house. The old **Assembly School**, now **St Columba's**, connected to the Established Church, lies on a grassy bank immediately to the south and is one of the village's oldest buildings, with the school opening in 1823. It is now a private house.

OLD ASSEMBLY SCHOOL

Further along the road and standing beside it is the old gate lodge to **Arnhall**, a substantial building set back behind the trees above and built in c.1901. There is no admittance to the house since it is privately owned. Its architectural inspiration is Edwardian rather than Arts and Crafts.

The road now passes **Bute Rock**. Under the cliff stands the building which, prior to 1881, served as the village post office. Note fixed to the wall an iron ring to which the postman of the time, Willie Currie, used to tether his horse.

You arrive next at **Mid Kiscadale**, the village centre. Opposite the square used to extend the longest pier on the Firth of Clyde. The first boat into the newly constructed pier was in 1899. The pier found its greatest use during the inter-war period with the tourist boom of those years. It was demolished during the 1960s and the former terminal buildings now form part of a builders' merchants, the building adjoining once being a tearoom. Nearby, note the small, castellated roofed building, the village shop. At one time this served as the local branch of the Bank of Scotland.

On the landward side of the square, at the top on the left, stands **Prospect House**. Now a dwelling, this was once the village Police House, with cells in the extension to the rear.

PROSPECT HOUSE

Just beyond the square, up a short access drive, stands the **Village Hall**. This was built by public subscription following a meeting convened by the British Legion in 1922 and was opened by the Duke of Montrose in 1926. It still belongs to the community and was fully refurbished in 1999-2000.

The village post office has moved several times. Having migrated from Bute Rock to the Cameronia, it then moved to **Ravensnest**, a fine house with sandstone bay windows situated just beyond the village hall and opposite the shop (no name on house). It is now in a building on the shore side of the road.

Continue on towards **South Kiscadale**, passing en route a single-storey building with bay windows and red-tiled roof. This was once the Co-operative Stores. **Grange House**, once a hotel and now a private house, stands just before the Art Gallery. It has nice 'baronial' touches and was constructed in 1895 after a fire had destroyed the previous building.

FORMER CO-OP SHOP

GRANGE HOUSE

Entering South Kiscadale, note the **Cooriedoon Care Home,** formerly the Whiting Bay Hotel, which stands partially hidden behind new houses. It can best be viewed, without intrusion onto private property, from the car park to the Eden Lodge Hotel. Elegantly constructed in sandstone, it dates from c.1900 and once incorporated an inn. It is believed to have been designed by the Burnett practice. It was converted to its present use in 1988.

Silverbank, a marine villa, is unmissable at the head of substantial lawns. Sadly it has lost its chimneys, but remains a finely proportioned building severely Georgian in style. It was built for a Captain Patterson during the 1770s. Crossing the Glenashdale Bridge, note the former Whiting Bay **Youth Hostel,** standing back from the road in its own grounds. This was previously the Easdale Boarding House and the 1891 Census Records show that it was built for a Miss McNicol.

SILVERBANK

The Cooper Angus caravan park is approached via an entrance whose incongruous pillars testify to the existence of a large house of the same name. The house, now demolished, was built c.1881 as a holiday residence for the politically prominent Duff Cooper family. The attractive **Duff Cottage** still stands to the south. The traditionally designed villa called **Carraig Dubh** ('Black Rock') after the stone outcrop on the shore opposite marks the official end of the village.

TOWARDS KILDONAN

Climbing the hill beyond Black Rock, the road passes through the small settlements of **Largymeanoch** and **Largybeg** towards **Dippen**. **Dippen Lodge** stands on cliffs overlooking the Ayrshire coast but the building, which is private, is not open to the public. It is of imposing Edwardian design, possesses some fine panelled rooms, and was constructed in the latter part of the 19th century as a shooting lodge for the south of the island. It is visible from the sea.

Further along on the right and just beyond the Kildonan turning, note **Grouse Lodge**, a gamekeeper's cottage with kennels to the rear. It dates from the late 19th century.
Return and descend towards Kildonan.

KILDONAN

The name 'Kildonan' derives from St. Columba's disciple St. Donan, who came to Arran with the great missionary in the 6th century to evangelise the Island. He is said to be buried close to the mill wheel at Kildonan Farm.

Descending towards the shore, come first to the complex of buildings on the left of the road, including the ruins of an old castle. The **Castle** was granted in 1406 by Robert III to his son, John Stewart of Ardgowan, passing down the Stewart line before being acquired by the Dukes of Hamilton. The ruins stand on private property, although they remain under the care of Historic Scotland. Of interest is that, at one time, a cobbler's shop used to occupy part of the building.

KILDONAN CASTLE

Back along the track, the old **Watch Tower** on the seaward side of a stand of trees was recently dismantled and, beyond where it stood to the north note some cottages. Lloyds of London established a signal station at Kildonan in 1882. A letter in the Ardrossan and Saltcoats Herald invited ships' captains to show signals when passing Malin Head, Rathlin Island and Kildonan, even at considerable distances. These stations were provided with powerful telescopes enabling flags to be read at up to twelve miles in good conditions. The trees were planted, not for shelter, but to provide a backdrop to the signaling platform, permitting the flags to be read more easily.

The **Coastguard Houses** were constructed upon the establishment of the coastguard station; one for the head coastguard and two additional ones, known as Lloyds' Cottages, for assistant coastguards and their families. Further accommodation was provided later nearer the watch-tower and rocket equipment shed. The station closed in 1981 and the service was transferred to Lamlash.

COASTGUARD HOUSES

A diversion may be made to view the privately owned **Kildonan Farm**. This lies down a track off the main road just before arriving at the Castle/Coastguard site. The farm occupies the site of a mediaeval chapel of which nothing now remains.

Further along the same track lies **Port Leek Farm** (in Gaelic 'Port na Leacain', meaning 'flat rocks' and very descriptive of the place). It was the birthplace of Captain Neil McKelvie, the father of Donald McKelvie of potato fame ('Broich', Lamlash q.v.). Captain McKelvie died in Calcutta at the age of thirty-eight and a model of his ship, the 'City of Corinth' can be seen in the Arran Heritage Museum in Brodick.

Returning to the main road, carry on past the coastguard cottages and descend into the village. On the shore stands the **Kildonan Hotel**, originally an inn dating from the late 18th century. In 1931 the owner added a large extension of seventeen bedrooms, seven of which had wash-basins, and three bathrooms, novel luxuries at the time on Arran. He gilded the lily by adding a sun lounge, a feature popular in the '30s. Owing to its remoteness, the hotel had its own supply of electricity.

Offshore can be seen the **Island of Pladda**, with its lighthouse a prominent feature. The lighthouse tower, ninety-five feet high, was built in 1790 by Thomas Smith and for many years there were three keepers and their families. It was the third lighthouse to have a fog signal, now no longer in use. The station was automated in 1990, the keepers withdrawn and the light remotely monitored from the Northern Lighthouse Board HQ in Edinburgh. The island, together with the redundant living accommodation and outbuildings, is owned privately.

In the middle of the village, pass on the right an imposing neo-colonial, porticoed and arcaded building, **Drimla Lodge**. This was built at the end of the 19th century to a South American design for the Clark family of Kilmarnock, the well-known shoemakers. It was refurbished during the 1970s when the balconies were replaced.

DRIMLA LODGE

Of other interest in the village is the **Yellow Port**, which Burrel identified during the 1770s as a safe landing place for passengers and goods. 'Puffers', small, coastal tramp steamers, were still unloading here until well into the 1940s. It was to this Port that all the materials for the building of Drimla Lodge were handled.

'The Hall' was opened in 1915 by Mrs. Clark of Drimla Lodge. It was built as a reading room, but found immediate employment as a centre for the ladies of the village to meet, knit and pack 'comforts' for the troops.

Kildonan Free Church and Manse were built after the 'Disruption' of 1843. People travelled great distances to attend and congregations were large, as many as seven hundred people attending Communion. Services ceased during the 1940s and the church later became a garage.

In 1771, the tenant of Drumlabarra Mill was Patrick McAlister, who had thirty-one families thirled to his mill (see Meal Mill, Cladach for explanation of thirling). Water to power the wheel at **Little Mill**, which stood where the road turns up the hill towards the main road, came from Loch Garbad. To distinguish Little Mill from the larger one at Torlin, it was known by that name, which in turn was applied to the whole district.

At the northwest end is the village stores, once **Cook's Stores**. The shop was opened in 1863 by the widow of John Cook in a small, thatched cottage. Her son William built new premises during the 1880s when many old cottages were being demolished or given extra storeys, dormer windows and slated roofs. The design of the stores resembled that of Ribbeck's (subsequently Alexander's) store in Brodick. In 1908 a telephone exchange was installed at the back of the shop and in 1937 it became the village post office.

Leaving the village by the north road, usually referred to as Church Brae, on the left stand the old **United Free Church and Manse**, now private houses. The church was opened for public worship in 1910 by Mrs. George Clark of Drimla Lodge, who, together with Miss Clark, gifted the organ. When the church closed in 1997 its bell was removed to the village hall.

UNITED FREE CHURCH

LEVENCORROCH

The main road now turns through northwest to north as one heads back up the west coast. After a short distance, looking to the right, the settlement on the skyline is **Levencorroch**. At the time of the Clearances the inhabitants wanted to rebuild along the road. The Estate refused permission for this and the old 'blackhouse' settlement pattern was modified instead. Since clachan buildings were usually constructed with the byres and steadings end-on to the houses and at the seaward end (Appendix 1), it is unusual to find in Levencorroch that they were rebuilt parallel to the shore.

Continue on and pass on the right the highest house on the island, once Bennan smiddy. The road now descends gradually, passing on the left the scattered settlement of **Shannochie**. Beside the road is a private house, converted from what was at one time the last thatched post office in Scotland. A phone box stands adjacent.

TORRYLINN AND KILMORY

As you enter **Torrylinn**, opposite the creamery, notice the newly restored building to the right of the road, **Ivybank**. This former small farmhouse, barn, byre, cottages and stables, were located originally near Kilmory Manse on the old road through the village. When the new road was built, the family demolished the entire farm stone by stone and rebuilt it where you see it today. This enabled them to see the 'comings and goings', which they regarded as highly important.

Just beyond Ivybank, turn right down the road towards **Kilmory Parish Church** and former manse now known as **Culanachaidh**. The latter is of particular interest. Although it is difficult to establish when the earliest manse was built on the site, part of the present building dates from the 17th century, possibly even from the Scottish Reformation in 1560. It may even have a claim to be the oldest inhabited manse in Scotland. A fire in the winter of 1710 destroyed the thatched roof and the front of the building, but sufficient remained for the front to be rebuilt in the Georgian style which you see today. The interior possesses several low doorways, a sure indication of pre-Georgian origins. The Church was built in 1785 on the site of an older structure.

KILMORY MANSE

KILMORY MANSE (Outbuildings)

KILMORY CHURCH

Return to the main road and, noting the old school on the right, descend the brae to **Lagg**.

LAGG

This settlement, effectively part of Kilmory, has a number of typical Arran buildings which have changed little over the centuries. **Lagg Cottage** stands just before the bridge on the right hand side. Asymmetrical in elevation, it was originally thatched.

Standing on the bridge and looking to your right beyond the cottage, it is possible to see the former **Flax Mill**, now a private house. There are records of it working as a flax mill from the early 1800s until its closure in 1861, although it almost certainly existed before then.

The **Lagg Inn** was built during the late 18th century and has been an integral part of Kilmory life for generations, appearing in island folklore as an inn where the 'jars' were refilled for 'The Wedding at Bennan' (see 'The Book of Arran' and 'The Isle of Arran', both by Robert McLellan). Added to the front facade during the 19th century were heavily decorated bargeboards, somewhat resembling similar features at Dougarie Lodge (q.v.).

LAGG INN

TOWARDS BLACKWATERFOOT

Climbing away from Lagg, set back on the right hand side is **Clachaig Cottage** known earlier as the **Gauger's House**. The 'gauger' was the excise officer for the Island during the 18th and 19th centuries. As might be imagined, he was not a popular man! The house is of neglected appearance but has several original features.

CLACHAIG COTTAGE

Further on, the road passes **Clachaig Farm**. Opposite the farm there stands a tall, largely windowless building. This was the kiln for the last licensed distillery on the island before the new one was built at Lochranza in the 1990s. It closed in 1836.

BENNICARRIGAN AND THE ROSS ROAD

At the **Ross Road** end there stands the former **Free Church**. This was built following the 'Disruption' of 1843 and during the period of great insecurity resulting from the Clearances and their accompanying social upheavals.

Drive along the Ross Road for about a mile and, opposite the quarry, note a farm steading. Part of the steading was the first house to be built after the 'Improvements' of the 1770s, during which the clachan of Bennicarrigan was cleared. The house, now Bogary Farmhouse, was used at one time as an outbuilding, but is currently being rebuilt. It was a typical Arran house in form, in which cottage, barn and byre formed one long structure. This differed from the more ancient 'blackhouse' pattern, with a central hole in the roof for the fire, in that it had fires at each end with chimneys in the gables.

A further half a mile on, where the road dips and turns, see on the right the ruins of **Glenree Mill**. This was a carding mill, where sheep wool was prepared for spinning by a process which teased out the fibres of the fleece. The mill worked until the end of the 19th century but only the stones survive as a reminder of one of the two carding mills on the Island, the other being at Glenshurig, near Brodick.

Isolated in the glen and about two miles beyond Glenree stands **Glenscorrodale Farm**. This now forms part of the Samye Ling Buddhist community dedicated to long retreats (see Holy Island). Although several of the outbuildings to this traditional farm have been retained, the farmhouse itself has been rebuilt. It may be of interest as being the childhood home of Jack McConnell, the First Minister for Scotland between 2001- 2007.

SLIDDERY

Sliddery is a much altered remnant of an old pre-Clearance clachan. Note the former school and schoolhouse, acting as such between 1860 and 1949 before becoming a shop and then a private house. Unusually, it still retains its original, school-like appearance.

Pass through **Corriecravie** and **Kilpatrick** and come to the junction with the **String Road**.

SHISKINE AND THE STRING

At this point, one can either turn right towards Brodick via the **String Road** through **Shiskine**, or, by turning left, continue through **Blackwaterfoot** and round the north end of the Island.

The **String Road** ('The String') was engineered in 1817 by Thomas Telford (1757-1855), the great engineer of canals and bridges throughout rural Scotland and of the Menai Bridge in North Wales. From the turning off the main island road, approaching the village of **Shedog**, come first to **St. Molio's Church** with its beehive gate pier. This is a fine example of the early work of J.J. Burnett and dates from 1888. Designed in a mixture of Gothic and Romanesque styles, with marked Arts and Crafts detailing, its porch and interior are especially interesting. It is said that Burnett's father had a hand in the design of the tower, pointing out to his son that the light, cavity wall construction proposed by him, resulting from his early training in France at the Beaux Arts, would not withstand Arran gales.

ST. MOLIO'S CHURCH

In **Shedog**, note the former **Hamilton Arms Hotel**. There had been an inn on this site since the late 18th century, although the present

ST.MOLIO'S CHURCH PORCH

building dates from the mid to late 19th century. It is now a private house, the former open space in front converted into a garden. Behind the hotel stood a meal mill, one of two operating in the village in 1878. It continued at full capacity until 1910 and then in a limited way until 1924. Threshing continued there until WW2.

HAMILTON ARMS HOTEL

Continue along the road, over the bridge at **Balnacoole** and through the modern settlement on the left, until you reach the **Balmichael Visitor Centre**. This is a conversion from the former Balmichael Farm, established on the site by the late 18th century. Most of the buildings are later than this and typical of the more prosperous farms on the island. Its best-known inhabitant was Colin ('Cole') Currie, who operated the horse brake over the String Road and, later in 1913, the first Arran bus service.

Two miles further on, at the junction with the **Machrie Road**, note on the right the carved stone pillar postbox. This was constructed in the mid-1870s for Dougarie Lodge (q.v.) by a local stonemason, David Wilson. At that time the Lodge had no mail delivery; letters were left at and collected from the box. The incised marks are not 'Celtic', but personal identifications by masons of their tools when commissioned from the blacksmith.

As you ascend the String, note the various farms set back against the hill on the left hand side - **Glaister**, **Monyquill** and, descending towards Brodick, **Glen Shurig**.

GLEN SHURIG FARM

65

Those wishing to extend their tour round the north end of the Island will have turned left at the String road junction and entered **Blackwaterfoot**.

BLACKWATERFOOT

Blackwaterfoot takes its name from the burn, the Black Water, which enters the sea at this point.

Passing the Blackwaterfoot Lodge Hotel, note on the right just before descending to the harbour **The Old Stables**. This was once a bus garage, then a coal store before being converted into a private house in the 1990s. Where the road bends right across the harbour bridge stands **Ferry Cottage** which, together with its accompanying store, was built in 1886. An adjacent weigh-house was demolished in the 1950s. The **Harbour** and stone bridge were rebuilt in their present form in 1900. Nearby, the **Kinloch Hotel** has been continually enlarged and re-modelled; it originated as a 19th century cottage. Behind the Ferry Cottage and reached by a short drive beside the burn stands **Victoria Lodge**, a fine Arts and Crafts villa dating from 1904. Until the 1990s when the rear was altered, it retained its original coach house and stabling.

VICTORIA LODGE

There are various houses of minor interest as you pass along the sea front. Note in particular **Cragg's House,** the last house on the right just before the golf club car park. This was built in the 1880s for Jane and Elizabeth Greig, unmarried sisters of private means, who later sold it to the Currie family.

CRAGG'S HOUSE

TORBEG

Climbing out of Blackwaterfoot, the road passes various small houses and **Shiskine Village Hall** before reaching the village of **Torbeg**. The Hall was formerly the United Free Church and was built in 1902, originally possessing a tower and steeple in its northeast corner. It was closed for worship in 1957.

At the road junction and war memorial (the road linking Torbeg to Shiskine is known as 'The Rodden'), note on the left the **Free Church Manse** built in 1847. The church itself was built in 1957 within the walls of the demolished former church dating from the same year as the manse.

FREE CHURCH MANSE

MACHRIE

Machrie may be approached from two directions, either travelling west across the String and turning right at the 'Celtic' pillar box, (q.v.), or from Torbeg.

Taking the 'String' approach, after crossing the first cattle grid and approximately five hundred yards beyond, note the pile of stones, which marks the spot where King Edward VII killed a stag. This gives a good vantage point to view the Standing Stones on Machrie Moor. Descending towards the sea, pass on the right at a bend in the road a substantial sandstone house with baronial embellishments and crow-stepped gables. This is **Machrie Farm House** (House of Machrie), built during the mid-19th century. Early in the 20th century it was decorated to a high standard and Edward VII took tea there after shooting his stag. At the time he was staying at Dougarie Lodge (q.v.).

MACHRIE FARMHOUSE

Crossing the golf course, come to the junction with the main shore road. **Machrie** is divided into four clachans: Tormore, Auchengallon, Auchencar and Dougarie. Auchengallon holds little of interest being much altered, but the others are worth further examination having retained much of their original character.

At the road junction, the house adjacent to **Weir's Garage** was at one time the village post office and dates from the late 19th century.

Should you have approached this point from Torbeg, you will have passed **Ashlar Farm** where another post office used to occupy the end cottage. Set back on the opposite side of the road stand good, unspoiled farm buildings. From Weir's Garage, proceed northwards, passing on the right the former schoolhouse, recently altered with a new central addition. At the next turning, take the track up to **Auchencar Farm** and the former clachan of Auchencar. Apart from the Sheepskin Shop, which occupies a byre with sloping floor, original stalls and sunken drain, note just beyond it **Rockmount,** a large 'cottage', built in 1900 in an Arts and Crafts style. This is an example of a house built to the restricted wall head height set by the Hamilton Estate; the high, steep roof in consequence is covering a much larger floor area than is usual in a traditional cottage. Alongside, in the ruins of the clachan, can be detected survivals of each stage era of Arran domestic building including walls constructed in both clay and lime mortar.

Return to the main road and proceed on to **Dougarie**.

DOUGARIE

Dougarie Lodge stands resplendent on the right hand side of the road, where the road curves round behind the **Boathouse**. This important building was erected in c.1850 as the principal shooting lodge for the 12th Duke of Hamilton. The word 'dougarie' derives from the Gaelic 'dubhgaradh' meaning rough black ground. The house is harled (rendered) and painted white but has been much simplified, the external walls originally having been decorated with antlers. There were red sandstone surrounds to the doors and windows and elaborate bargeboards (see Lagg Inn). In "Castles in the Air", Lady Jean Fforde's account of her early life on Arran, she describes Dougarie as being 'all eaves and valleys and gables and verandahs and pointed, mullioned windows and pointed doors'. Note also the tower with crow-stepped gables. The garden was laid out within a castellated folly, built as a ruin in 1905 to the design of James Mather.

Dougarie retains its exterior outbuildings designed for sport and recreation, including an ornate **Game Larder** reminiscent of the Bavarian Summer House at the Castle (q.v.), the **Keeper's House**, converted from a farmhouse into a castellated folly and the **Boathouse** on the seaward side of the road.

The **Boathouse** is attributed to J.J. Burnett, who was later to design alterations to the Lodge which were never implemented. Built in the local sandstone, it has a remarkably stylish presence, with its sweeping rooflines, Gothic trefoil bargeboards and intimations of an oriental teahouse. The building was commenced in 1884 and completed a year later, the structural engineer being Thomas D. Weir of Glasgow. The plan of the building is interesting. The central part was used as a gaming room, where guests who were not out on the hill shooting could enjoy the day. To each side of the centre were spaces for the rowing boats used to ferry guests out to the Duke's yacht, 'The Thistle'. The interior is decorated with cartoons by Prosperi and Spy of guests who stayed at The Lodge.

NOTE: The gardens and boathouse are open twice a year during the summer.

DOUGARIE LODGE

BOATHOUSE AT DOUGARIE LODGE

Continuing north along the coast, after about two miles and on the hill to your right it is possible to see, vegetation permitting, the remaining two houses of the large clachan of **Balliekine** or **Banlicken** where the 1891 Census listed a total of 35 residents. The clachan was the last on the island to use the agricultural 'run-rig' system, whereby plots of land were rotated and relocated annually for cultivation by each member (Appendix 1). The clachan cemetery lies on the shore, protected by a large stone dyke, and is accessible via the Imacher to Whitefarland shore walk.

IMACHER

Where the road turns away from the shore and climbs steeply, at the top of the brae, come to **Imacher**. Note **Hazelwood**, a late 19th century farmhouse, handsome with its fireclay tabbed window surrounds and doors and windows with octagonal glazing patterns. At one time the farmhouse was a Temperance Inn used by islanders awaiting the ferry to Carradale in Kintyre. Temperance Inns were common on Arran until the 1940s. It is possible to walk up the adjacent track and, passing on your left a fine Estate cottage, **Cnoc na Coille,** to reach Banlicken and enjoy the fine views across the Sound to Kintyre.

HAZELWOOD

Return to the main road and continue through **Whitefarland**, one of the original three shore clachans, to **Pirnmill**.

PIRNMILL

Originally the clachan of **Penrioch**, the settlement was located half a mile up the hill to the northeast and away from the shore. But in the late 18th century it was discovered that local trees provided wood suitable for the manufacture of 'pirns', or bobbins, for use in the cotton thread mills. Between 1780 and 1840 a lively trade developed, pirns being supplied to the mills of E.P. Clark (later J & P Coats) of Paisley and the new village of 'Pirnmill' grew up along the shore, displacing Penrioch. By 1840, however, all the trees had been harvested and the business failed. The **Mill** for manufacturing the pirns was built about 1780, beside the burn in the village. It has now been converted into two private dwellings. It was powered by an overshot water wheel in which the water from a runnel was delivered to the top of the wheel. The runnel still exists and can be seen.

It is of interest that, although no pier was built at Pirnmill, steamers from Campbeltown and Glasgow used to call to transport the finished pirns and passengers to the mainland, a large rowing boat being used to ferry goods and people out to the waiting steamer. The first regular ferry service is recorded as taking place in 1848, this continuing until WW2.

The former **Church of Scotland** in the middle of the village was built in the Arts and Crafts style. Originally it was the United Free Church and was constructed in 1910 as a memorial to the Reverend John Kennedy of Lennimore, a popular preacher of the time.

Towards the northern end of the village, standing in a corner of a field, is the present Church of Scotland, originally the **Free Church**. The building was erected in 1920, possibly as a church hall, and is a prefabricated corrugated iron building, its interior lined in yellow pine. Such prefabricated buildings, schools, halls and churches were made by various companies in Scotland, such as Speirs & Co. of Glasgow and Charles D. Young and Co. of Edinburgh, and could be ordered from catalogues.

The Pirnmill example is of particular interest since it is in such good condition and is still being used for its originally intended religious purpose. Brodick Church Hall and Lamlash Village Hall are other examples of this form of construction.

FORMER FREE CHURCH

Leaving the village, pass on the right **Thundergay**. This part-ruined clachan sits on the hill above the beach and a number of the houses are still occupied. The large, prominent Victorian villa on the hillside to the south, **Wellside,** was built in the late 19th century.

CATACOL

Coming over the second set of 'humps' and round the corner, **Catacol** lies at the back of the bay. Approaching the village, leave the car, cross the Catacol Burn and walk along the road on the right hand side. Half way between the burn and the village you will see nestling behind the stone dyke the remains of a building containing three metal 'barking' pans, essentially large versions of the clothes washing pans common in Victorian laundries. These, together with the crumbling stone walls, are all that remain of a **Barking Shed or**

Barking House, one of two remaining on the island (the other is at Lochranza).

The function of the barking shed was to soak fishing nets in a mixture of water and the extract from a tannin-rich bark to increase their weight, to preserve them and to prevent shellfish becoming attached. Originally oak bark, this was replaced by the more effective 'cutch', the product of a species of *Acacia*, especially the *Acacia catechu*. At Catacol, the boats were brought close to the shed by way of a canal from the burn and the nets taken in and treated in heated vats. Of interest is that many of the brown sails often seen in oil paintings of the Victorian period would have been dyed with cutch.

BARKING SHED

Continue on to the village, viewing at a distance **Catacol Farm House**, recently restored. This was built as a shooting lodge for Lord Rossmore, husband of the 8th Duke of Hamilton's illegitimate daughter Ann Douglas, who was gifted the lands from Machrie to

Catacol as a wedding dowry. The couple were childless so the lands reverted to the Duke in 1854.

The row of twelve cottages along the shore, known familiarly as **The Twelve Apostles**, was built at c.1850 for crofters cleared from the run-rig clachan in Glen Catacol, Abhainn Bheag, to make way for sheep and game. However, they refused to live in the new cottages, as there was no land attached. The houses lay empty for two years until gradually the inhabitants drifted back and acquired skills other than farming, including fishing, but for a long time they suffered deprivation and the terrace was known as 'hungry row'. Of interest is that each cottage had a differently shaped window in the gable facing the sea, the variation making it possible for fishermen out in Kilbrannan Sound to recognise their homes.

TWELVE APOSTLES

At the **Catacol Bay Hotel**, note the steeply pitched gables to the front, typical of many Arran villas dating from the later 19th

century. The building was originally the manse for the church at Lennimore which no longer exists.

Continuing towards Lochranza, pass on the right a solitary late 19th century villa. Of particular interest is the back-house on the north side. This illustrates clearly the type of miniature dwelling built on Arran to accommodate the owners of the main houses during summer letting.

VILLA AND BACKHOUSE NEAR LOCHRANZA

LOCHRANZA

Originally, **Lochranza** was populated from the many runrig farms from the glen and surrounding hills after they had been cleared, but later, until the end of the 19th century, it became one of the principal fishing ports on the west coast of Scotland, with almost four hundred fishermen making a living from the herring. Hence, it became the favoured retirement village for the island's seafarers. Its popularity as a retirement haven accounts for the many substantial villas lining the southern shore, most dating from the late 19th and early 20th centuries. Note in particular **Benvaren, Kincardine Lodge, Daisyknowe** and **The Anchorage**. The Burrell Journal gives a sketch of where the 99-year lease for the Wee Anchorage was given in the late 18th century.

BENVAREN

DAISYKNOWE with BACKHOUSE

THE ANCHORAGE

Sited on a promontory into the sea loch stand the ruins of **Lochranza Castle** (see page 6), whose history is summarised on the adjacent Historic Scotland board. The Castle was mentioned by Fordum in 1400 as one of the two royal castles on Arran and during the 16th century it became the stronghold of the Montgomeries.

NOTE: The castle is open throughout the year

Nearby stands the former **Free Church** building, constructed in c.1900 in the Arts and Crafts style. It is now a private residence.

Standing on a large, isolated site amongst trees is an architecturally important building, the **Lochranza Youth Hostel**. Formerly this was the Lochranza Hotel. A report in the Arran and Saltcoats Herald (A & SH) in August 1895 states: "built to order of the Duke of Hamilton. Mr. Burnett was the architect; very neat and modern with covered area and balconies". So the plans for the hotel may have been drawn up by J.J. Burnett in 1893-4. The original scheme was much larger than what you see today; only part of what was intended was built. Much later the modern additions to the west were added. Note the typically 'romantic' Arts and Crafts detailing of the bays, gables, chimneys and dormer windows.

LOCHRANZA YOUTH HOSTEL

At the head of the loch, just before the left turn across the golf course to the Newton Shore and set back from the road, stands the second **Barking Shed**. The function of barking sheds has already been described (Catacol q.v.), but the Lochranza one is of particular interest owing to its relative completeness, although now in a poor condition. The building dates from the 19th century and noteworthy are the means of entry to an upper level by way of stone steps and the remains of the canal by which boats could be brought up at high tide.

BARKING SHED

Further along the road on the right stands an ornate **Lych Gate**, dating from the 1930s and with an inscription internally, leading to **St. Bride's Church**. The original church dates from 1550, just before the Scottish Reformation, and it is the oldest church on the island still in regular use. At first it had a thatched roof but, after its reconstruction by the Duchess Ann in 1712, this was replaced by slates. Further additions and alterations were made in 1795. Note the timber lined interior giving the visitor the impression of being in an upturned boat and the circular, stained glass window gifted in 1931 in memory of the Reverend John Colville. Outside, in the original door opening to the rear, see Grizel Fraser's monument with skull and crossbones.

Entry to the church may be gained with keys available from the Field Study Centre nearby.

ST. BRIDE'S CHURCH

Cross the causeway to the **Newton Shore** and note the fine 18th century building with 19th century additions to the west end. This is **The Lodge**, built about 1750. Burrell's Journal in the 1770s states that two brothers, both Captain Robertson, built the track to the slate quarries above Glen Farm. It is probable that one of the brothers had The Lodge built for his own occupation.

THE LODGE

Cross back to the main road and continue on south. On the left stands the unassuming but sensitively designed **Golf Club House,** erected between the two world wars, and, towards the end of the village on the right, the **Distillery**, built in 1996 to designs by the architects David Hutchison & Associates.

LOCHRANZA DISTILLERY

TOWARDS SANNOX AND CORRIE

Leave the village and cross the pass known as **The Boguillie**, noting on the hillside on the left as you climb the **Keeper's Cottages** with kennels. Ruined settlements all along the east side of the North Sannox burn were supposedly the most populated part of pre-Clearance Arran. Descending and before reaching Sannox, turn left towards the North Sannox picnic site. From here there is a good shore walk, best undertaken during the morning before the sun moves round, to the 'fallen rocks', an old landslide. The white post supporting lights which you pass en-route is one of several **navigation beacons** used to measure the speed of new ships doing the 'measured mile' down the Firth of Clyde; a second may be seen in lower Glen Sannox.

A short distance beyond the landslide there lies in a bowl in the hills the ruins of the clachan of **Laggantuin**. Enough remains of this for the visitor to appreciate the relationship of the cottages to the 'inbye' and 'outbye' lands separated by their 'dry stane dykes' (dry stone walls).

SANNOX AND CORRIE

Descending the hill into **Sannox**, on the right across the fields can be seen sheep pens and a ruined hayloft, all that remains of a former clachan cleared for sheep. Further on, on the right, stands **Sannox House**, a good example of an 'improvement' farmhouse with extensive outbuildings.

At the bend in the road, just before the bridge, a track leads up to **Sannox Congregational Church** and **Manse**. The two buildings were erected in c.1820 as a result of the efforts of the Reverend Alexander McKay, who had been appointed to the Island in 1806. A grant of land was made by the Duke of Hamilton and the buildings were erected at a cost of £400, the money being raised by subscription. Some seven years later, however, the Duke persuaded the inhabitants of Glen Sannox with an offer to contribute towards fares, to emigrate in order to make way for agricultural improvements and larger more efficient farms. It was in this chapel that the islanders cleared from the clachans attended divine service for the last time before sailing for a new life in Canada.

Note the simply designed interior, the sundial standing nearby with carved date of 1813, intriguingly predating the church. **Dundarroch**, next door, was once a stable but converted into a house for Allan Cameron, who was ordained pastor in 1878.

SANNOX CHURCH

Along a private drive leading from the church approach stands **Woodside Cottage**, once an Estate house but now a private residence. It can be best seen from the shore walk between Sannox and the North Sannox picnic site.

WOODSIDE COTTAGE

Return to the main road, cross the bridge and enter the village. On the right, opposite the first car park, stands **Glen Cottage**, once a tearoom and managed during the 1930s by the owners of the Corrie Hotel. Beside it a track leads into Glen Sannox, where the ruins of the **Barytes mine** may be seen. Barytes, or more correctly barium sulphate, was used in the manufacture of paint and is still useful as a lubricant for oil and gas drilling. The mine was opened in 1840 and over 5000 tons of ore were mined between 1853 and 1862 before the workings were closed by the 11th Duke of Hamilton to preserve the beauty of the surroundings. Unexpectedly, the mine had a brief new life following WWI; owing to a national shortage of barytes, the mine was reopened and continued in operation until 1938, by which time the ore was exhausted. To assist extraction and export, a tramway and wooden pier were built, both demolished after WW2.

Further along the road the **Granite Jetty** was constructed to permit the shipment of granite blocks. On the right there is a succession of houses with histories, built in a variety of styles. These include **Ferghan Mhor**, once the village school, and **Gowanlea**, where in 1877 Alexander and Archibald McKillop set up their joinery and boatbuilding business.

FERGHAN MHOR

GOWANLEA

Entering **Corrie**, there are several interesting detached houses in the first part of the village, among them **Tigh na Achaidh**, a single-storey house dating from the 1930s with some nice Art Deco touches.

Corrie School was built in 1870 by the Duke of Hamilton to accommodate sixty pupils. It was extended in 1898 to take as many as one hundred and thirty pupils, an indication of how populous the village then was. The adjacent house for the urgently required female teacher 'had to proceed immediately'.

CORRIE SCHOOL

Next door stands **Corrie Church**, the first known commission for the practice of J. Burnett and Son on the Island and dating from 1885. It is plainer than St. Molio's (q.v.), entirely Gothic and possessing a severe simplicity of form, which suggests the hand of John James Burnett's father, John, who was still active at that time.

The porch and interior are nicely detailed, although not yet possessing the full Arts and Crafts flourishes.

CORRIE CHURCH

The row of cottages just beyond the church is well known as **Port Street** and high above, overlooking the harbour, stands the **Congregational Church Hall**, built in 1898 and now a private house.

The harbour, known as 'The Port', picturesque with its quaint form and giant sandstone and granite block construction, was connected to the limestone industry, which was carried on up the hill to the right opposite the harbour head. The remains of the limekilns may still be seen. Later, Neil Paton built boats there, his boats being named after ocean liners.

Beyond the harbour, set in a gentle crescent, the next row of cottages is well known as **High Street**. Originally thatched and single storey, they were built between 1860-70 and were recorded in the 1891 Census.

HIGH STREET CORRIE VILLAGE

At the sharp right-hand bend just beyond High Street, note on the left the timber shed on stilts. This was part of the ferry operation and was intended for the safe keeping of passengers' luggage. The ferry sailed from opposite Craigmhor where there is a small inlet. Note the grooves cut in the rock to accommodate the timbers for the landing.

FERRY HUT SHOWING PORT STREET

91

Immediately after this stand **Corrie House** and the **Corrie Hotel**. The former is an attractive villa with many windows facing the sea and detailed in the Arts and Crafts style. The **Hotel**, a well-proportioned, red sandstone building on a prominent site, was built in the 1850s to replace the inn at Cladach (q.v.) after that ceased to trade.

CORRIE HOUSE

CORRIE HOTEL

Past the art shop and behind a stone wall and gardens, **Cromla** was one of the original marine villas on Arran. It was built in the 1770s by Miss Grizel (Grace) Baillie, on land leased to people of independent means for 99 years. The form of the house, building materials and situation were agreed with the Hamilton Estate. (A full description of materials and accommodation in the original villa including a 'necessary house' can be seen in the Burrel Journal). The Baillies were frequent visitors to Arran and were connected by marriage to other prominent Ayrshire landowners such as the Cunninghames, Reids and McCreadies. In 1810 the house came into the possession of Robert McCreadie, who enlarged it imaginatively by placing an extension in front of the original and giving it the neo-classical form which can be seen today. Among its many interesting features is an outdoor washhouse with chimney carved from the sandstone cliff beside the burn running through the garden. It was probably made for Dr McCreadie by the same mason who carved out for him the 'doctor's bath' which can be seen on the shore. In 1921, Cromla was adopted as the manse for Corrie Parish Church (q.v.), but reverted to private ownership in 1957 after the Corrie and Brodick churches were united.

CROMLA

Continue on through the village, past the row of attractive sandstone villas of which **Averton**, with its stone backhouse and **Woodlands** are perhaps the best examples. Next come to the former **Free Church** set back amongst a stand of conifers. Now a private house, it was built in 1894. It never had a resident minister, visiting preachers boarded in Aranmhor, the house next door.

AVERTON AND ITS BACKHOUSE

WOODLANDS

FORMER FREE CHURCH

95

At the rear of the new villa to the north of Aranmhor there stands a castellated stone **Folly**. It is said that this was built as a gun emplacement by a ship's captain, enabling him to fire a salute as Queen Victoria sailed past in 1876 on her way to inspect the fleet. There is no public access.

Heathfield, an elaborately barge-boarded Victorian villa, can be seen at the head of the short drive to the south of the Free Church. This was built by the blacksmith David Craig, whose smiddy lay behind Corrie House (q.v.). Later, it became a hotel and tearoom.

HEATHFIELD

Alpine, a fine sandstone villa standing behind the second harbour known as the **Sandstone Quay**, was constructed for the quarry master James King. The Quay was built in 1882 for the shipment of sandstone, a major Arran export during the latter part of the 19th century. The strange arrangement of blocks at the end of the quay behind the inappropriately sited public toilets is not just a random pile of leftover stones. Their purpose was to shelter vessels tied up at the quay from southerly gales. Unfortunately they have much reduced in recent years, having been bulldozed or uplifted.

ALPINE

Corrie Terrace, a 1960s development of council houses, acquired its name from an earlier row, unusually two stories high, built during the 19th century to house quarry workers. Nearby lies the quarry. A large amount of sandstone was quarried in Corrie during the 19th century, it being valued for its density and consistency. It was used in the construction of Troon harbour, of many Glasgow tenements and of Kinloch Castle on the island of Rhum. In 1881 there were twenty-two men employed under the quarry master James King. The old quarry office existed until 2009, converted into as private house Lichfield.

Immediately before leaving the village, past the road end to High Corrie, note the nicely detailed, freestanding villa, **Craigard**, set back behind neat lawns and wrought iron railed fence.

HIGH CORRIE

High Corrie is approached via a track at the south of the village marked with a green 'Goatfell' sign. Park in the lower car park opposite The Steading, climb the track and bear right at the fork just beyond the upper residents' car park. The clachan is remarkable in that its footprint is little altered since it was surveyed in 1813 for the Duke of Hamilton by Bauchope before the Arran Clearances took place. It is one of the few remnants of the pan-European, ancient Celtic communal farming system in which settlements were placed half way between the hill land and the shore, the land being held communally with the work shared out amongst the inhabitants. It has been held that High Corrie represents a missing link between prehistoric agricultural settlements and the later clachans.

High Corrie is designated by Historic Scotland as being of outstanding historical interest. Observe that the houses have similar orientations, approximately gable-on to the sea. Where there are two or three cottages in row form, the lower ones at the seaward ends were originally the byres. Note the spaces between the dwellings which are important parts of the settlement pattern: the small central meadow or green, the 'erratic' (a large boulder dating from the retreat of the glaciers) and, outwith the settlement proper, the remains of runrig fields and turf dykes.

Since the 1813 survey, two cottages have been demolished, only the foundation stones remaining, and a cottage of wood construction was replaced by a modern one in 1985, carefully designed to blend in. Gables were rebuilt to take chimneys and clay mortar has been replaced by lime, thatch by tarred felt or slate and one or two dormers have been added but, with these exceptions, what you see is what was originally built. That it has survived is a miracle when, down the centuries, so many other settlements have disappeared. It is therefore of great importance in the social history of Scotland and an appropriately high note on which to end this survey of Arran's buildings.

HIGH CORRIE GENERAL VIEW

HIGH CORRIE FINLAYS COTTAGE

SUGGESTED USEFUL ORGANISATIONS

The Architectural Heritage Society of Scotland, Edinburgh
The Arran Civic Trust
The Isle of Arran Heritage Museum
The Scottish Civic Trust
The Scottish Vernacular Buildings Working Group

FURTHER READING

Campbell, K.T.S., *Arran: a History* (Birlinn Ltd., 2007)
Farquharson, Maureen (ed), *Isle of Arran Heritage* (Arran Graphics, 2002)
Fforde, Jean, *Castles in the Air Stuart* (Titles Ltd., 1996)
Fforde, Jean, *Feet on the Ground: from Castles to Catastrophe* (Glasgow, 2001)
Inglis, James C., *Brodick Old and New Arthur* (Guthrie & Sons Ltd)
McLellan, Robert, *The Isle of Arran* (David and Charles, 1970)
Mackenzie, W.M., *The Book of Arran, Vol. 2: History and Folklore* (The Arran Society of Glasgow, 1914)
Naismith, Robert J., *Buildings of the Scottish Countryside* (Gollancz, 1985)
S.W.R.I. Arran Federation, *History of the Villages of the Isle of Arran* (2002 revd.)

APPENDIX 1: THE CLACHANS OF ARRAN

Clachans, communal farms which varied in population from twenty to two hundred people, were originally part of the pan-European, ancient Celtic communal farming system. The runrig clachans and their way of life survived the feudal system until the end of the 18th century. They possessed the following significant features:

Considerable ties of kinship existed between families.

The land surrounding the settlement was held under a system of tenure known as 'runrig', which was not only a method of cultivation but also described a system whereby farmers within the clachan possessed plots of good, medium and indifferent quality. On Arran, for the sake of fairness, farmers drew lots annually to ensure equitable rotation of the good and poor land.

The better land was found usually close to the cluster of houses (the 'inbye' land) and the poorer quality further away (the 'outbye' land).

Some of the land was held in common, such as that immediately round the houses and on the mountain or moor.

Under the feudal system, the mountain land was allocated in 'soumings', a souming entitling a farmer to graze a cow or so many sheep; the number of soumings a farmer held depended on how much of the inbye or outbye land he possessed.

On Arran the largest clachans were in the south end of the island.

APPENDIX 2: JOHN BURREL AND ROBERT BAUCHOPE

During the 18th century, the Agricultural Revolution transformed the face of farming throughout Britain. It was slow to arrive on Arran, but during the early decades of the 19th century it arrived on the Island where its proponents sought to replace the ancient system of run-rig (Appendix 1), whose social advantages were offset by the depletion over time of the fertility of the soil. Any money available which might have been used to improve the soil was lost in successively higher rents.

In the mid-1770s, when the 7th Duke was still a minor, **John Burrel** was commissioned by the Trustees of the Estate to make suggestions as to how the estate's income might be improved. Burrel had practical experience gained from working on large estates and was familiar with up to date farming practices. He made a detailed inventory in his Journal of the farms and tenancies, paying much attention to efficiency and productivity and little to the people whose land his reforms would affect. He suggested the rationalisation of farm holdings into larger, single-tenanted farms and the enclosure of land. Those tenants, who could not afford the higher rents charged by the Estate to increase the land's profitability, were to be removed. The result of the reforms was a reduction in the numbers of tenants, security of tenure being further reduced by the principle of competitive tenancies.

Burrel was also one of the first to advocate leases to wealthy mainlanders wishing to have homes on the island to increase the revenue to the Estate. Two of the houses built on land with 99-year leases as a result of this development were **Cromla** in Corrie and **Seafield** in Lamlash. John Burrel did not live to see the full implementation of his schemes, but his Journal with its findings and 'suggestions' for improvements has reverberated round Arran ever since.

Robert Bauchope, factor and surveyor to the Duke of Hamilton, came to Arran in about 1812 and was resident on the island for many years. He repeated Burrel's survey and, following similar principles, suggested dividing the farms between a smaller number of tenants and removing the run-rig system in its entirety (Appendix 1). When this was done, however, it became apparent that the rationalisation did not work as well as expected: the farms continued to be uneconomic, since the land could not support even the reduced number of tenants, who were in competition instead of co-operation, as in the old run-rig system. Previous to 1815 the ducal property had been set in 113 farms each having four to twelve tenants. After that date, the division was into 458 farms, of which 53 were large and the others of between two and forty acres. Further consolidation occurred to increase the sizes of the smallest farms and sub-division was strictly prohibited.

Bauchope pursued the Improvements for the next twenty years firmly and systematically, creating larger, single-tenanted farms of between 100 and 400 acres with the remaining tenants being mostly cleared from the land. The Estate also built large farmhouses, which it maintained, and created a number of small lots which were made available for rent. On these, however, tenants had to build and maintain their own houses, dykes and fences and enclose the land with ditches and hedges. Other restrictions were imposed: sheep were prohibited except on stock farms, goats banned entirely and herds of swine no longer allowed to roam free. The whole character of farming on Arran changed completely. In Glen Sannox, for example, twenty-seven families had to make way for a single farm and throughout the Island dispossessed people were forced to leave to take work where they could find it, many in the burgeoning smokestack industries of Glasgow. Others emigrated, many going to Canada.

South, Mid and North Sannox were cleared in 1829 to make way for a single large sheep farm at Mid Sannox and a smaller enclosed sheep farm at the Cock of Arran. Catacol was cleared in 1863 in favour of deer, which at that time were more profitable than sheep. The north of the island in the second half of the 19th century was a mixture of deer forest and grouse moor, whilst the very north end was mostly sheep

APPENDIX 3: SIR JOHN JAMES BURNETT, ARCHITECT

John James Burnett (1857-1938) was born in Glasgow in 1857, the youngest son of John Burnett (1814-1901), a successful architect. He was educated in Glasgow and later in Paris, where he enrolled with Jean Louis Pascal at the Ecole des Beaux-Arts. He gained the Diplome du Gouvernement in 1876 before touring Italy. From his earliest days his work revealed a mastery of plan and elevation, a deep understanding of stone-cutting and the love of sculpture which typified his later work.

Burnett's first work was the Fine Art Institute in Glasgow, the commission for which he won in competition in 1878. At this early stage he was much influenced by the teaching he had just received and the building was distinguished by its combination of Greek with French Renaissance influences. This was followed by The Clyde Navigation Trust building of 1882-6. Burnett was admitted to membership of the Royal Institute of British Architects in 1881 and in the same year he made a second tour of Italy. The following year his father took him into partnership, the practice thenceforward being known as John Burnett and Son. They were joined in 1882 by John Archibald Campbell.

In 1886, Burnett married Jean Marwick, a classic late Victorian beauty, and in a kind of 'annus mirabilis' in the same year the practice established an international reputation by winning the competition for the Edinburgh International Exhibition. This was a very Beaux-Arts building, highly sculptural in treatment, but both Burnett and Campbell soon discovered that, whereas such effects were appropriate for public buildings, they had to be more adaptable for private clients.

Between 1886-9, the practice was joined by a third graduate of the Beaux-Arts, Alexander Paterson, the younger brother of James Paterson the French-trained Glasgow School painter, who demonstrated great skill as a watercolourist. This proved extremely useful when presenting the designs for the **Duke of Hamilton's**

Arran Estate in the 1880s. A cause of contention in the office at this time was not only the lack of cost-consciousness of the younger partners, but also the foreign detailing and insubstantial structural ideas brought over from Paris. The tower to **St. Molio's Church, Shiskine,** had to be redrawn several times before it would satisfy Burnett senior as to its strength and stability in the island climate.

The elder Burnett retired in 1890 at the age of seventy-five, after which the practice's design approach changed radically. Burnett and Campbell realised that, if they were to have any hope of winning commissions in London, they would have to produce designs which appealed to London-based assessors such as Waterhouse. This took Burnett into the then fashionable world of the neo-Baroque. As a result he undertook another study tour in Germany and Italy in 1895. By 1900, this style had become the common language of Glasgow building.

In 1896, the Burnetts visited the USA for the first time to study laboratory and operating theatre design, but Burnett had become interested in American contemporary domestic architecture at least a decade earlier and now saw for himself the low-profiled, big-roofed, broad-eaved designs which, upon his return, he adapted to his ecclesiastical work. Many of his church designs from this period show squat, pyramid-roofed towers and mixed Romanesque and late-Gothic detailing; they were a low, easy-to-heat alternative to the tall, Early English style in which the practice earlier specialised.

In 1897 Burnett's partnership with John Campbell was dissolved by mutual consent and a new change in the direction of Burnet's work took place. In 1903-4, Burnett was selected to design the new Edward VII Galleries at the British Museum and in 1905 he established a London base from which the commission was carried out. Other London commissions followed and Burnett began spending less and less time in the Glasgow office. Upon the completion of the Edward VII Galleries, Burnett received a knighthood and the bronze medal of the Paris Salon, followed by the gold in 1922.

Work continued in both Glasgow and London on numerous commissions, but relations with new partners, in particular with Thomas Tait, and assistants marred relationships. Honours continued to flow in, principal amongst which were the award of the Royal Gold Medal in 1923 and election as a Royal Academician in 1925. Despite failing health, he was often appointed as assessor for schemes submitted for competitions, culminating in his appointment to the international jury for the League of Nations Building in Geneva in 1927.

Burnett retired gradually, financial circumstances making it necessary for him to retain an interest in the practice, although appearing in the London office only twice a year for business meetings. He died in 1938 in Surrey at the age of eighty-one.

The following is a list of the buildings completed by the practice of John Burnett, Son and Campbell between 1885 and 1900 on the Island of Arran:

c. 1884	Boathouse at Dougarie Lodge (attribution only)
1885	Established Church, Corrie
1888	St. Molio's Church, Shiskine
after 1889	House, Whiting Bay
1893	Hamilton Terrace, Lamlash
1894	Proposed additions to Dougarie Lodge, Dougarie. They were never carried out.
1894	Youth Hostel, Lochranza, formerly the Lochranza Hotel. A large scheme was proposed initially, but a reduced one carried out
1894	Village Hall, Brodick
after 1896	Hotel(s) at Whiting Bay
1899	Dalgorm, Lamlash
1899	Rose Cottage, Lamlash (known as 'The Nurse's House')
late 1800s	Made in Arran' Crafts shop, Lamlash
1899	Waiting room at Brodick pier, now demolished (attribution only)

NOTES

NOTES